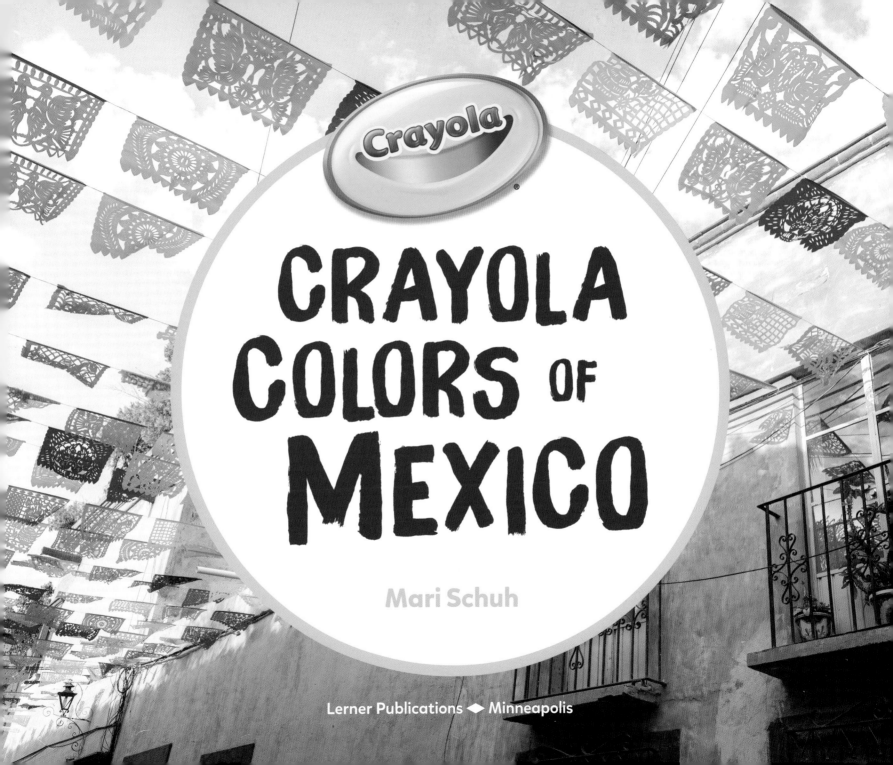

Crayola

CRAYOLA COLORS OF MEXICO

Mari Schuh

Lerner Publications ◆ Minneapolis

For Leah, a great reader

Content consultant: Xóchitl Bada, Associate Professor, University of Illinois at Chicago

Lerner Publications Company
An imprint of Lerner Publishing Group, Inc.
241 First Avenue North
Minneapolis, MN 55401 USA

For reading levels and more information, look up this title at www.lernerbooks.com.

Main body text set in Mikado Medium.
Typeface provided by HVD Fonts.

Library of Congress Cataloging-in-Publication Data

Names: Schuh, Mari C., 1975– author.
Title: Crayola colors of Mexico / Mari Schuh.
Other titles: Crayola country colors.
Description: Minneapolis : Lerner Publications, [2020] | Series: Crayola country colors | Includes bibliographical references and index. | Audience: Ages 5–9. | Audience: K to Grade 3. | Summary: "Visit the colorful country of Mexico with Crayola! With pink feathered flamingos, bright blue ocean waters, vibrant dancing dresses, and more, explore the colors found in nature and culture all across Mexico"— Provided by publisher.
Identifiers: LCCN 2019016936 (print) | LCCN 2019980686 (ebook) | ISBN 9781541572645 (library binding) | ISBN 9781541587175 (paperback) | ISBN 9781541582736 (pdf)
Subjects: LCSH: Colors—Juvenile literature. | Crayons—Juvenile literature. | Mexico—Juvenile literature.
Classification: LCC F1208.5 .S35 2020 (print) | LCC F1208.5 (ebook) | DDC 972—dc23

LC record available at https://lccn.loc.gov/2019016936
LC ebook record available at https://lccn.loc.gov/2019980686

Manufactured in the United States of America
1-46531-47576-6/10/2019

TABLE OF CONTENTS

LET'S VISIT MEXICO!

Mexico is full of bright, beautiful colors.

It's a big country in North America.

There is so
much to see
in Mexico!

LOOKING AROUND

The sun shines on aqua ocean water and tan, sandy beaches.

Mexico is between the Pacific Ocean and the Gulf of Mexico.

The land has beaches, mountains, volcanoes, forests, and more!

Emerald grass grows near tall pyramids in Mexico.

These pyramids are very old.

They are made of tan stone.

COLORFUL ANIMALS

Look in the trees and see **yellow**, **green**, **red**, and **orange**.

A bright toucan lives in the rain forest.

Coral flamingos
wade in warm water.

Jaguars are covered in **orange**-and-**black** fur.

Their markings help them hide in Mexico's forests.

CELEBRATIONS AND FOOD

Pink, **yellow**, and **red** flash by in a parade!

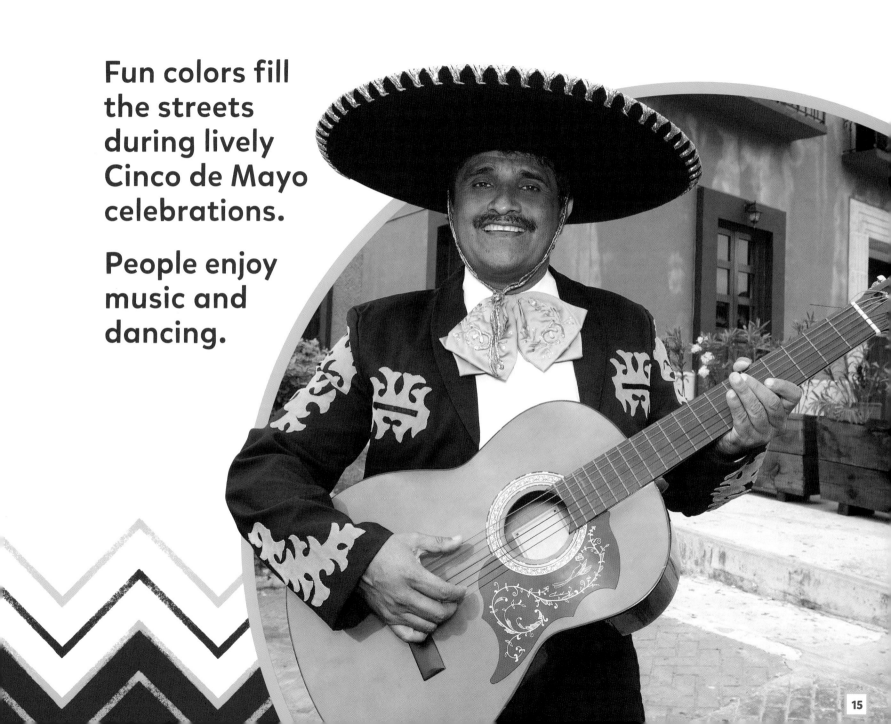

Fun colors fill the streets during lively Cinco de Mayo celebrations.

People enjoy music and dancing.

During Day of the Dead, people in Mexico remember loved ones who have died.

They decorate special altars with candles, flowers, and food.

The holiday is a joyful time filled with color.

Spicy **red** peppers and juicy **orange** papayas grow in Mexico.

People enjoy yummy tacos.

Meals in Mexico are bursting with color!

MORE ABOUT MEXICO!

Continent: North America
Capital city: Mexico City
Population: 125,959,205 (2018 estimate)

ARCTIC OCEAN

NORTH AMERICA

EUROPE

ASIA

ATLANTIC OCEAN

Mexico City

Mexico

AFRICA

PACIFIC OCEAN

PACIFIC OCEAN

SOUTH AMERICA

INDIAN OCEAN

AUSTRALIA

SOUTHERN OCEAN

MANY COLORS

There are so many colors in Mexico. Here are some of the Crayola® crayon colors used in this book.

MIDNIGHT BLUE

AQUAMARINE

GREEN

ALMOND

WILD STRAWBERRY

GLOSSARY

altars: raised platforms or tables used as the center of a ceremony

celebrations: ceremonies or gatherings on special days

Cinco de Mayo: a Mexican holiday that is celebrated on May 5. Cinco de Mayo celebrates the Mexican army's victory over the French army in 1862.

Day of the Dead: a holiday celebrated in Mexico and around the world that honors the dead

markings: spots, stripes, and patches of color on an animal's fur

North America: the continent that includes the United States, Canada, Mexico, and Central America

Pacific Ocean: the ocean that is west of North and South America and east of Asia and Australia

pyramids: large structures made of stone with sides shaped like triangles

rain forest: a thick forest that gets a lot of rain

TO LEARN MORE

Books

Dean, Jessica. *Mexico.* Minneapolis: Jump! 2019.

Moon, Walt K. *Let's Explore Mexico.* Minneapolis: Lerner Publications, 2017.

Nelson, Robin. *Crayola ® Cinco de Mayo Colors.* Minneapolis: Lerner Publications, 2019.

Websites

Crayola: Cinco de Mayo Shaker Craft
https://www.crayola.com/crafts/cinco-de-mayo-shaker-craft/

National Geographic Kids: Mexico
https://kids.nationalgeographic.com/explore/countries/mexico/

INDEX

PHOTO ACKNOWLEDGMENTS

Image credits: Will Zinn/Shutterstock.com, p. 1; Photogilio/iStock/Getty Images, p. 4 (church); arturogi/iStock/Getty Images, p. 4 (tops); minisothic/Shutterstock.com, p. 4 (flower); good 4 nothing/Moment/Getty Images, p. 5 (top); sljones/Shutterstock.com, p. 5 (right); Jesse Kraft/EyeEm/Getty Images, pp. 6–7; Genna88/Shutterstock.com, pp. 8–9; Ondrej Prosicky/Shutterstock.com, p. 10; OGphoto/iStock/Getty Images, p. 11; Frans Lanting Studio/Alamy Stock Photo, pp. 12–13; Photo Researchers/Science Source/Getty Images, p. 14; LUNAMARINA/iStock/Getty Images, p. 15; stockcam/iStock/Getty Images, pp. 16–17; lunamarina/Shutterstock.com, pp. 18–19; Steve Allen/Shutterstock.com, p. 20 (flag); Laura Westlund/Independent Picture Service, p. 20 (map).

Cover: Ondrej Prosicky/Shutterstock.com (toucan); Byelikova Oksana/Shutterstock.com (skulls); www.infinitahighway.com.br/Moment/Getty Images (beach); bpperry/iStock/Getty Images (city); AleSal/iStock/Getty Images (cactus).